Anthology of Post-Tonal Music

D1085781

This collection of 41 selections and excerpts represents a wide range of music from the 20th century. Designed for use with *Understanding Post-Tonal Music* by Miguel Roig-Francolí, it can also stand alone as an anthology for study and analysis in other music theory courses.

Miguel A. Roig-Francolí is Distinguished Teaching Professor of Music Theory and Composition at the University of Cincinnati College-Conservatory of Music.

Anthology of Post-Tonal Music

For use with Understanding Post-Tonal Music

Miguel A. Roig-Francolí

College-Conservatory of Music University of Cincinnati

Routledge
Taylor & Francis Group

NEW YORK AND LONDON

Custom edition published 2020
by Routledge
52 Vanderbilt Avenue, New York, NY 10017

and by Routledge
2 Park Square, Milton Park, Abingdon, Oxon, OX14 4RN

Routledge is an imprint of the Taylor & Francis Group, an informa business

© 2020 Taylor & Francis

First published by McGraw-Hill, 2008

Library of Congress Cataloging-in-Publication Data
Library of Congress Control Number: 2010560304

ISBN: 978-0-367-43285-0 (pbk)

Bembo
Taylor & Francis, ltd

Contents

Preface

This anthology is meant to be used in conjunction with the study of the textbook *Understanding Post-Tonal Music*. The book includes detailed analyses of a total of thirty-two pieces by twenty-five composers, ranging chronologically from Claude Debussy and Igor Stravinsky to Kaija Saariaho, Augusta Read Thomas, and Thomas Adès. All these thirty-two pieces are included in the anthology. Whenever possible, complete pieces or movements have been used. If a composition or movement is particularly long, a substantial and representative fragment has been chosen for analysis and inclusion in the anthology. The remaining nine compositions in the anthology are used for analytical assignments in the textbook. The total number of pieces in the anthology is thus forty-one, by twenty-six composers. Because of the close relationship between the book and the anthology, the latter is not meant to be an optional supplement to the book, but rather an essential and required component of the pedagogical packet.

The exact correspondence between book chapters and anthology pieces is as follows:

Chapter 1. Pitch Centricity and Composition with Motivic Cells

Analysis 1.1. Debussy, "La cathédrale engloutie," from *Preludes*, Book I (Anthology no. 1)

Analysis 1.2. Stravinsky, Introduction to Part I, from *The Rite of Spring* (Anthology no. 4)

Anthology nos. 2 and 3 are used for assignments.

Chapter 2. Pitch Centricity and Symmetry

Analysis 2.1. Bartók, "Song of the Harvest," from *Forty-four Violin Duets* (Anthology no. 5)

Analysis 2.2. Bartók, "Whole-tone Scale," from *Mikrokosmos*, vol. 5 (Anthology no. 6)

Anthology nos. 7 and 8 are used for assignments.

Chapter 3. Introduction to Pitch-Class-Set Theory

No pieces from the anthology are used in this chapter.

Chapter 4. Analyzing Atonal Music

Analysis 4.1. Webern, "Five Movements for String Quartet," op. 5, III (Anthology no. 10)

Analysis 4.2. Schoenberg "Angst und Hoffen," no. 7 from *Book of the Hanging Gardens*, op. 15 (Anthology no. 11)

Anthology nos. 9 and 12 are used for assignments.

Chapter 5. Drawing on (and Reinterpreting) the Past . . .

Analysis 5.1. Stravinsky, *Agnus Dei*, from Mass (Anthology no. 13)

Analysis 5.2. Hindemith, Interlude in G, from *Ludus tonalis* (Anthology no. 14)

Anthology no. 15 is used for an assignment.

Chapter 6. . . . And Inventing the Future

Ives and Musical Borrowing (includes a discussion of Anthology no. 16, Charles Ives's "The Things Our Fathers Loved," from *114 Songs*)

Analysis 6.1. Ives, "The Cage" (Anthology no. 17)

Analysis 6.2. Crawford, *Diaphonic Suite* no. 4, III (Anthology no. 18)

Chapter 7. Twelve-Tone Music I: An Introduction

Analysis 7.1. Dallapiccola, "Contrapunctus secundus," from *Quaderno musicale di Annalibera* (Anthology no. 19)

Analysis 7.2. Dallapiccola, "Quartina," from *Quaderno musicale di Annalibera* (Anthology no. 20) Anthology no. 21 is used for an assignment.

Chapter 8. Twelve-Tone Music II: Invariance, Symmetry, and Combinatoriality

Analysis 8.1. Webern, Piano Variations, op. 27, II (Anthology no. 22)

Analysis 8.2. Schoenberg, *Klavierstück*, op. 33a (Anthology no. 23)

Chapter 9. Serialism: Developments After 1945

Analysis 9.1. Stravinsky, "Lacrimosa," from *Requiem Canticles* (Anthology no. 24)

Analysis 9.2. Boulez, *Structures Ia* (Anthology no. 25)

Analysis 9.3. Babbitt, *Composition for Twelve Instruments* (Anthology no. 26)

Chapter 10. Expanding the Limits of Musical Temporality

Analysis 10.1. Messiaen, Introduction, from *Turangalîla Symphony* (Anthology, no. 27)

Analysis 10.2. Musical Characters in the Second String Quartet, I (Anthology no. 28)

Analysis 10.3. Stockhausen, *Stimmung* (Anthology no. 29)

Chapter 11. Aleatory Music, Sound Mass, and Beyond

Analysis 11.1. Cage, *Winter Music* (Anthology no. 30)

Analysis 11.2. Lutosławki, *Jeux vénitiens*, I (Anthology no. 31)

Analysis 11.3. Ligeti, *Ramifications*, mm. 1–38 (Anthology no. 32)

Chapter 12. Where Past and Future Meet . . .

Analysis 12.1. Rochberg, *Music for the Magic Theater*, reh. 1–17 (Anthology no. 33)

Analysis 12.2. Berio, *Sinfonia*, III (Anthology no. 34)

Anthology no. 35 is used for an assignment.

Chapter 13. Simplifying Means

Analysis 13.1. Reich, *Violin Phase* (Anthology no. 36)

Analysis 13.2. Andriessen, *De Staat*, mm. 1–161 (Anthology no. 37)

Analysis 13.3. Pärt, *Cantus* (Anthology no. 38)

Chapter 14. Into the Twenty-First Century

Analysis 14.1. Thomas, *Spring Song* (Anthology no. 39)

Analysis 14.2. Adès, *Asyla*, II (Anthology no. 40)

Analysis 14.3. Saariaho, *Ariel's Hail* (Anthology no. 41)

The organization of the anthology thus follows the organization of the textbook, which is designed according to a roughly chronological plan and, within that, by general topics. This modular organization following two simultaneous criteria acknowledges that twentieth-century music is best understood not only in technical terms, but also in a historical context, and that stylistic and compositional developments do not take place in a historical vacuum.

An initial general topic, pitch centricity, covers music by Debussy, early Stravinsky, and Bartók in Chapters 1 and 2. The next topic, atonal music, is covered in Chapters 3 and 4. In Chapter 3, pitch-class sets are studied formally, setting the stage for the analyses of Webern and Schoenberg atonal pieces in Chapter 4. Chapters 5 and 6 discuss two seemingly contradictory, yet highly complementary, stylistic trends: neoclassicism, as found in the music of Stravinsky and Hindemith, and ultramodernism, as found in Ives and Crawford. Chapters 7 and 8 are devoted to the study of "classical" twelve-tone music, with reference to works by Dallapiccola, Schoenberg, Berg, and Webern, and Chapter 9 deals with serial practices after World War II, as illustrated by Stravinsky, Boulez, and Babbitt.

Chapter 9 thus provides a link between music before and after World War II. Post–World War II music is covered in the last six chapters (9 through 14). The general topics in these chapters, and following serialism, are issues of temporality (Chapter 10, including analyses of music by Messiaen, Carter, and Stockhausen), aleatory composition, sound mass, and other post-serial techniques (Chapter 11, with reference to Cage, Lutosławski, and Ligeti), quotation and collage (Chapter 12, with focus on Rochberg and Berio), minimalism (Chapter 13, which includes analyses of music by Reich, Andriessen, and Pärt), and finally a review of some of the most recent compositional trends as found in pieces by Thomas, Adès, and Saariaho (Chapter 14).

Miguel A. Roig-Francolí
College-Conservatory of Music
University of Cincinnati

1. Claude Debussy (1862-1918)

"La cathédrale engloutie," no. 10 from *Preludes*, Book I (1910)

Dans la sonorité du début

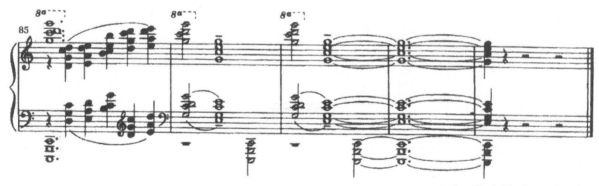

⟨...La Cathédrale engloutie⟩

2. **Claude Debussy**
"Canope," no. 10 from *Preludes*, Book II (1910-13)

6

3. Claude Debussy
"Sarabande," from *Pour le piano* (1894-1901)

4. Igor Stravinsky (1882-1971)
Introduction to Part I, from *The Rite of Spring* (1913)

17

19

21

5. Béla Bartók (1881-1945)

"Song of the Harvest," no. 33 from *Forty-four Violin Duets* (1931)

6. Béla Bartók

"Whole-tone Scale," no. 136 from *Mikrokosmos*, vol. 5 (1932-39)

7. Béla Bartók
"Diminished Fifth," no. 101 from *Mikrokosmos*, vol. 4 (1932-39)

8. Béla Bartók

"From the Island of Bali," no. 109 from *Mikrokosmos*, vol. 4 (1932-39)

9. Anton Webern (1883-1945)

Five Movements for String Quartet, op. 5, II (1909)

10. Anton Webern
Five Movements for String Quartet, op. 5, III (1909)

11. **Arnold Schoenberg (1874-1951)**
"Angst und Hoffen," no. 7 from *Book of the Hanging Gardens*, op. 15 (1909)

daß mein La - ger Trä - - - nen schwem - men, daß ich je - de

Sehr langsam

Freu - de von mir weh - re, daß ich kei - nes Freundes

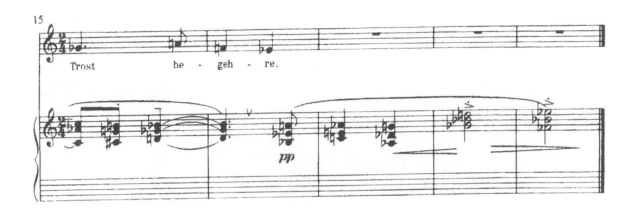

Trost be - geh - re.

Translation of Text

"Anguish and Hope," by Stefan George

Anguish and hope in turn seize me.
My words trail off in sighing.
Such tempestuous longing assails me
That I do not turn to rest or sleep
That tears flood my couch,
That I ward off every pleasure,
That I seek no friend's consolation.

12.   Alban Berg (1885-1935)

"Schlafend trägt man mich," no. 2 from *Four Songs*, op. 2 (1908-1909)

Translation of Text

"In Sleep I am Borne," by Alfred Mombert

In sleep I am borne unto my homeland.
From afar I come, over peaks, over abysses
Over a darkened sea unto my homeland.

13. Igor Stravinsky (1882-1971)
Agnus Dei, from Mass (1944-48)

Translation of Text

Lamb of God,
Who takes away the sins of the world,
Have mercy upon us.

Lamb of God,
Who takes away the sins of the world,
Have mercy upon us.

Lamb of God,
Who takes away the sins of the world,
Give us peace.

14. Paul Hindemith (1895-1963)
Interlude in G, from *Ludus tonalis* (1942)

15. Paul Hindemith
"Vom Tode Mariä I," from *Das Marienleben* (1923)

und hob ihr Antlitz auf____ zu dem und dem.... (O Ursprung na-men-lo-fer Trä - - -

- - - - - - nen-bä-che.)

Wie zuerst

Sie a - ber leg - te fich in ih-re Schwä - - che und zog die

Him - mel an Je ru - - fa-lem fo nah her - an, daß ih - re

See - - le nur, aus-tre-tend, sich ein we-nig strecken muß - - te, schon hob

er sie, der al - - - - - - les von ihr wuß - te,

hin - ein in ih - re gött - - - - -

- li - che Na - tur.

Translation of Text

"On the Death of Mary," by Rainer Maria Rilke

The same great angel which had earlier brought her tidings of her conception, stood there, waiting until she noticed him. And he spoke, "It is now time that you appear." And she was frightened as before and, humbly acquiescing, became again as the maiden. Then he became radiant and, nearing her infinitely, vanished as into her face. And he called together the widely dispersed Disciples to the house on the slope, the house of the Last Supper. They came gravely and entered fearfully. There she lay, along the narrow bedstead, mysteriously immersed in her end and in her chosen state—entirely unharmed, as one unused, listening to the song of angels. Now when she saw them waiting behind their candles, she tore herself from the abundance of voices and, with a full heart, gave away the two robes which she owned. And she raised up her countenance to this one and that one. . . (O source of nameless streams of tears.) Then she sank back in weakness and drew the heavens so near to Jerusalem that her soul, setting forth, had only to stretch itself a little, for He who knew everything about her was even then raising her to her godly nature.

16. Charles Ives (1874-1954)
"The Things Our Fathers Loved," from *114 Songs* (ca. 1917)

17. Charles Ives
"The Cage," from *114 Songs* (1906)

NOTE:- All notes not marked with sharp or flat are natural.

18.   Ruth Crawford Seeger (1901-1953)
Diaphonic Suite no. 4, III (1930)

55

19. Luigi Dallapiccola (1904-1975)

"Contrapunctus secundus," no. 5 from *Quaderno musicale di Annalibera* (1952-53)

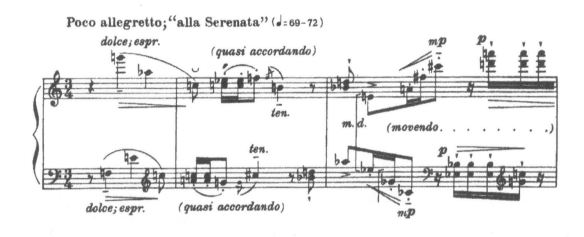

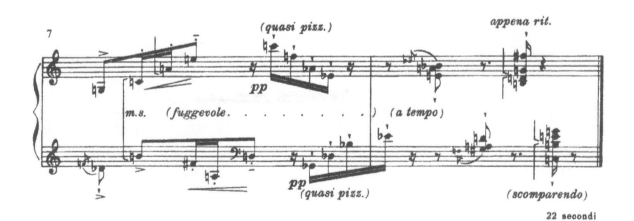

22 secondi

20. Luigi Dallapiccola
"Quartina," no. 11 from *Quaderno musicale di Annalibera* (1952-53)

21. Anton Webern (1883-1945)

"Wie bin ich froh," no. 1 from *Drei Lieder*, op. 25 (1935)

blühn— die Blu-men mir die Welt!— noch ein-
world— is o - ver - grown with flow'rs!— Once more

mal— bin ich ganz ins Wer-den hin-ge-stellt
I— in cre-a - tion's por-tal live my hours,

und bin auf Er-den.
and yet am mor-tal.

ca 1'

60

22. **Anton Webern**
Piano Variations, op. 27, II (1935-36)

23. Arnold Schoenberg (1874-1951)
Klavierstück, op. 33a (1929)

24. Igor Stravinsky (1882-1971)
"Lacrimosa," from *Requiem Canticles* (1966)

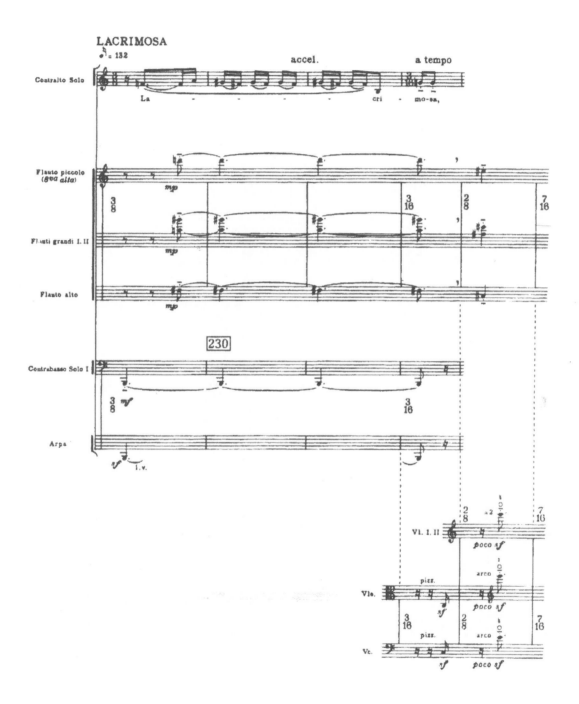

N.B.: All instruments in this score are notated in C.

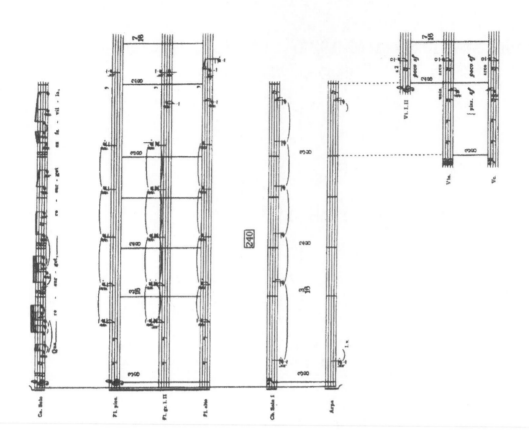

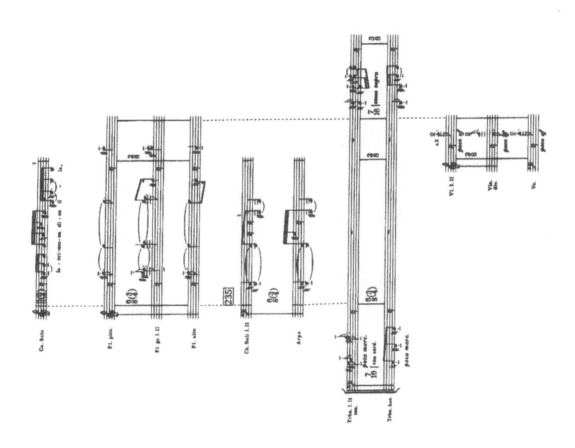

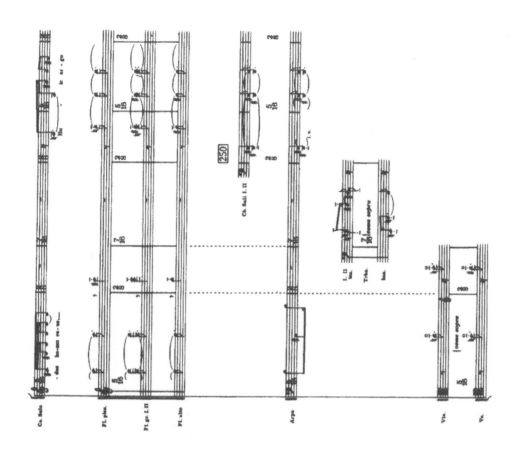

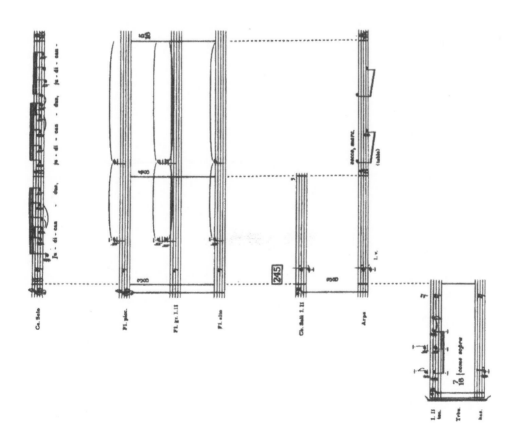

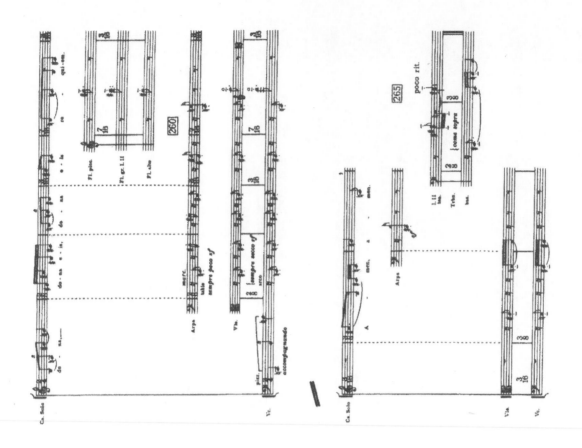

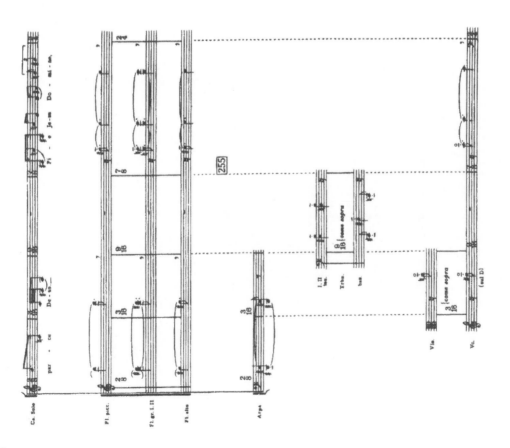

Translation of Text

On that day full of tears,
When from the ashes arises
Guilty man to be judged,
Spare him, O God.
Merciful Jesus, Lord,
Grant them eternal rest.
Amen.

25.   Pierre Boulez (b. 1925)
Structures Ia, mm. 1-39 (1952)

73

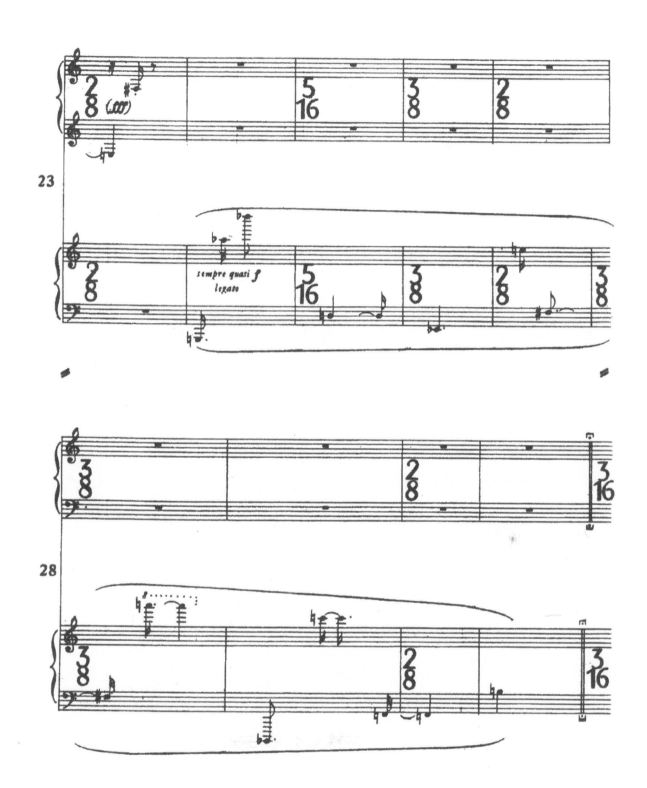

26. Milton Babbitt (b. 1916)

Composition for Twelve Instruments, mm. 1-26 (1948)

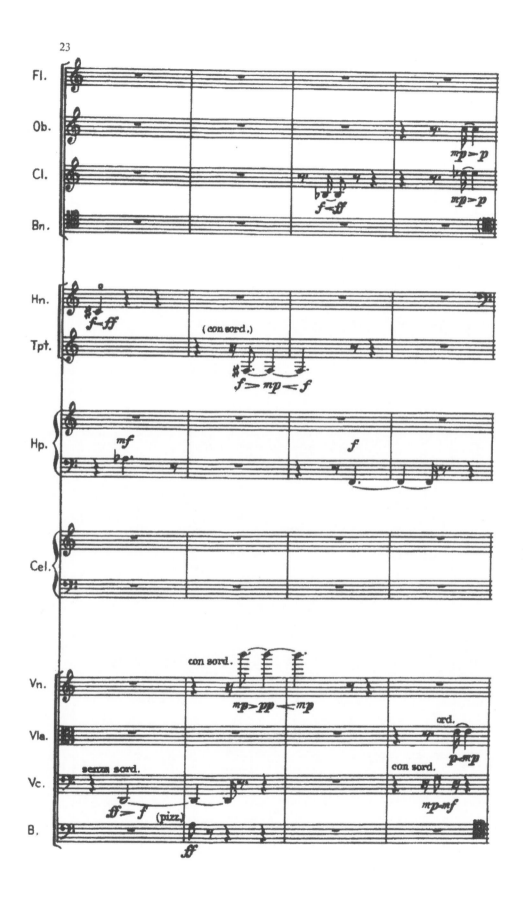

27. Olivier Messiaen (1908-1992)
Turangalîla Symphony, Introduction, reh. 12-22 (1946-48)

91

97

100

28. Elliott Carter (b. 1908)
String Quartet no. 2, I, mm. 35-134 (1959)

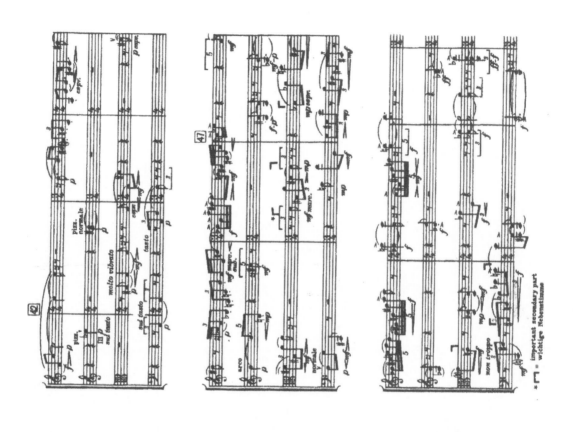

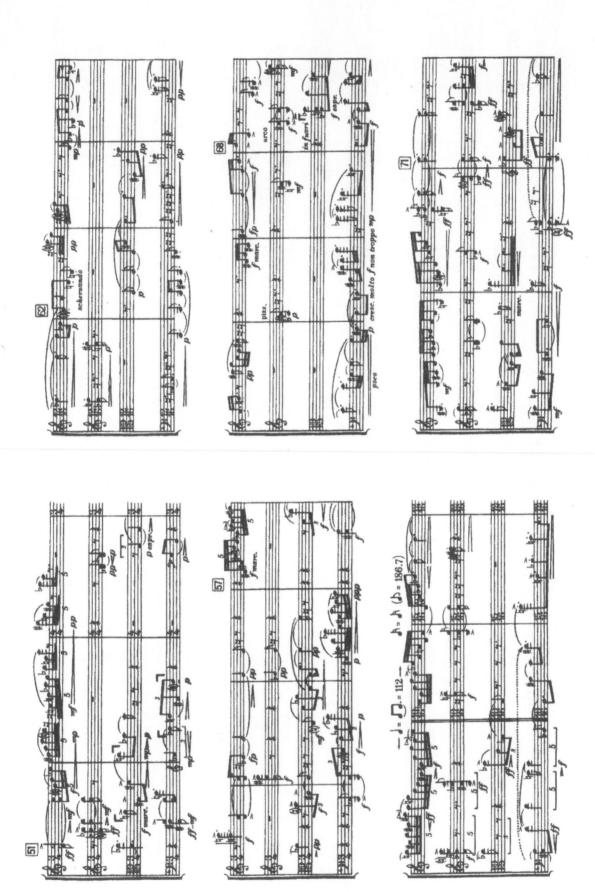

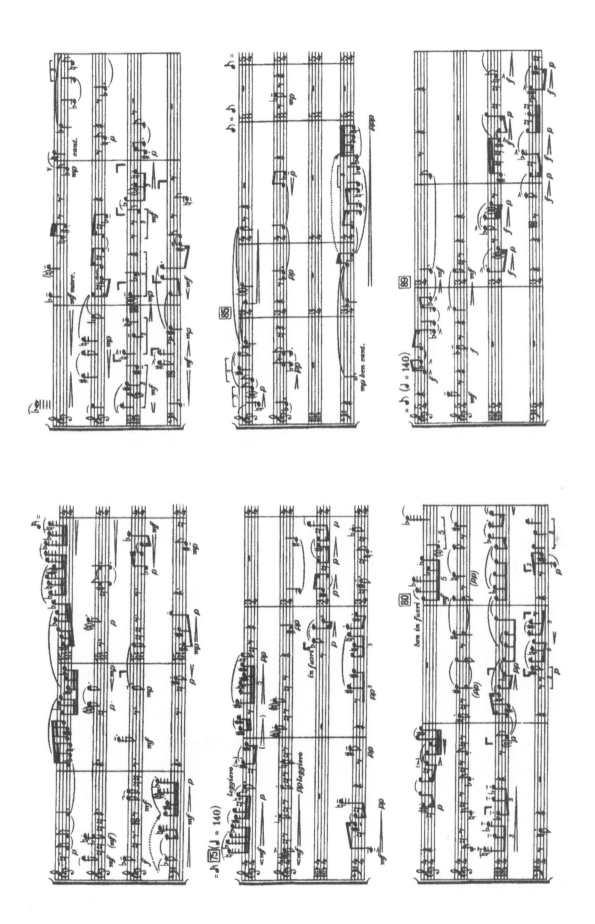

105

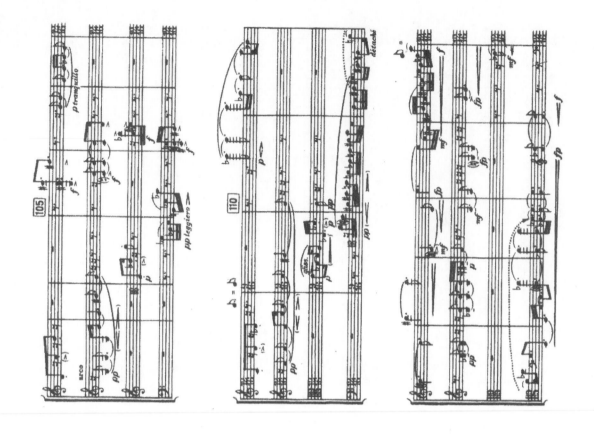

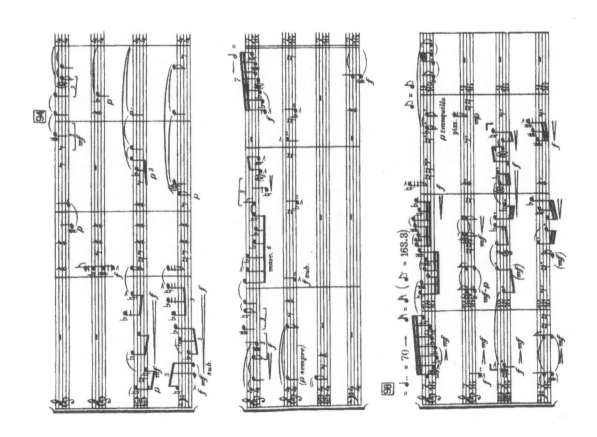

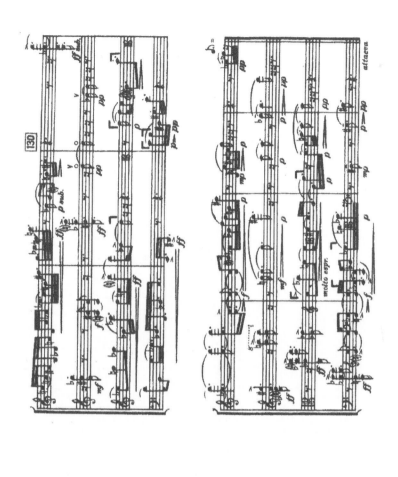

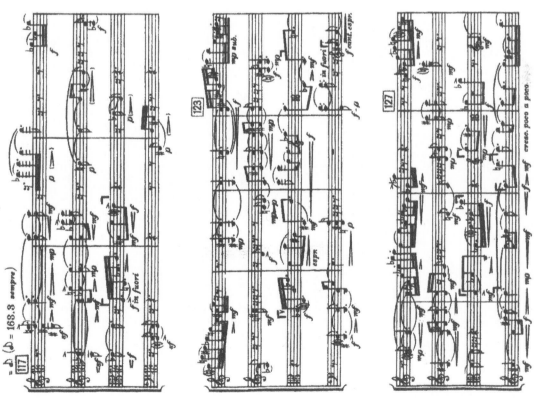

29. Karlheinz Stockhausen (b. 1928)

Stimmung (three pages: *Formschema*, one sample page of *Modelle*, and one sample page of *Magische Namen*) (1968)

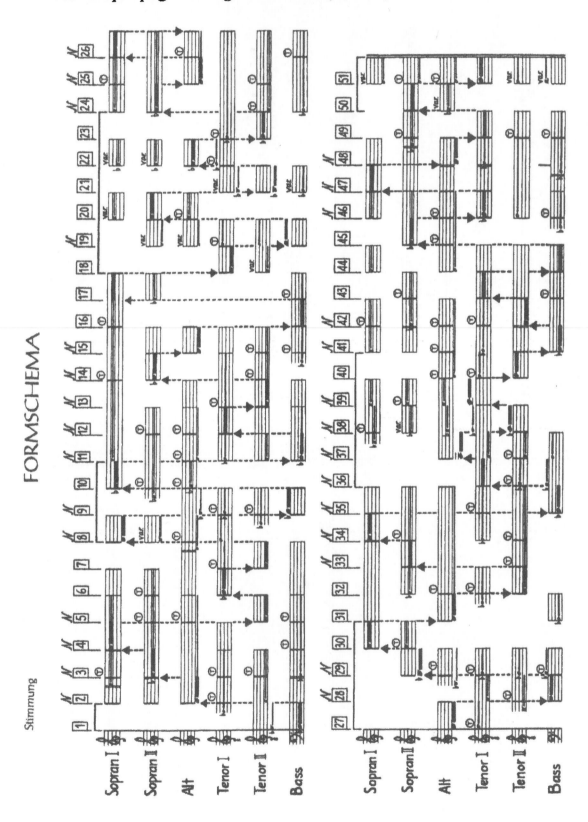

Stockhausen
STIMMUNG

Modelle

Männernamen.

109

Magische Namen

RHEA Griech.: Mutter von Zeus	**AEOLUS** Griech.: Gott der Winde	**URANOS** Griech.: Gott des Himmels
CHRONOS Griech.: Gott der Zeit	**DIANA** Röm.: Jagdgöttin	**DIONYSOS** Griech.: Gott der Fruchtbarkeit, besonders des Weinbaus
ZEUS Griech.: König der Götter	**VENUS** Röm.: Göttin der Liebe	**POSEIDON** Griech.: Gott des Meeres
GAIA Griech.: Erdgöttin		
HERA Griech.: Beschützerin der Frauen und der Ehe		

30. John Cage (1912-1992)
Winter Music (one page) (1957)

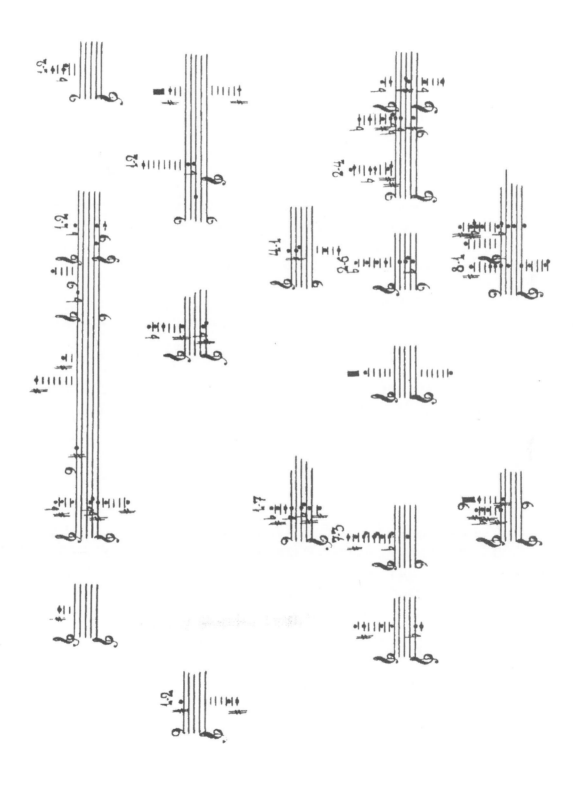

31. Witold Lutosławski (1913-1994)
Jeux vénitiens, I (1960-61)

N.B.: All instruments in this score are notated in C.

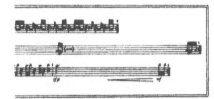

ought not to be played from the beginning but from any other phrase between two caesuras. Each musician should play his part with the same freedom as if he were playing it alone: the rhythmic values serve only as a guide and the basic tempo is between ♪ = 140 and ♪ = 150

Sections B D F H:

The bar lines, rhythmical values, and metre are intended merely for orientation: the music should be played with the greatest possible freedom. The number of notes at places like the third bar of section B in the first viola part depends on the strength of the player's bowing (spiccato or preferably ricochet). In section D the first violin part should be played independently of the conductor and the rest of the ensemble.

Reihenfolge der Wiedergabe: A B C D E F G H

Abschnitte A C E G:

A wird von der Holzbläser- und Schlagzeuggruppe gespielt. C von Holzbläsern, Pauken und Schlagzeug. E von Holzbläsern und Blechbläsern. F von Holzbläsern, Pauken und Schlagzeug G von Holzbläsern, Blechbläsern, Pauken, Schlagzug und Klavier. Die durchbrochenen „Taktstriche" mit Zäsurzeichen darüber verlangen Zäsuren von beliebiger Dauer; je nach Dauer der Zäsuren wird das Klangbild dichter oder lockerer erscheinen. Spieldauer der einzelnen Abschnitte: A = 12'', C = 18'', E = 6,'' G = 24'' Der Dirigent gibt die Zeichen für Beginn und Schluß eines jeden Abschnittes (der Abschlag für Abschnitt A gilt gleichzeitig als Einsatz für B, der Abschlag für C als Einsatz für D usw.)

Beim Abschlag eines jeden Abschnittes sollen die Musiker ihr Spiel sofort unterbrechen. Hat ein Musiker einen entsprechenden Part bereits vor diesem Zeitpunkt beendet, wiederholt er ihn vom Beginn des betreffenden Abschnitts an. Die folgenden Abschnitte, nacheinander durch Buchstaben C E G bezeichnet, sind so zu verstehen, daß

die einzelnen Stimmen nicht von Anfang an sondern von irgendeiner anderen Phrase zwischen zwei Zäsuren gespielt werden sollen' Jeder Musiker führt seinen Part so frei aus, als ob er ihn allein spiele; die rhythmischen Werte dienen nur als Anhalt, das Grundtempo liegt zwischen ♪ = 140 und ♪ = 150

Abschnitte B D F H:

Taktstriche, rhythmische Werte und Metrum dienen lediglich als Orientierungshilfen, die Musik soll so frei wie möglich gespielt werden. Die Anzahl der Noten an der Kraft des Bogenstriches ab (mit Springbogen oder besser ricochet) Im Abschnitt D soll die 1. Violine ihren Part unabhängig vom Dirigenten und dem übrigen Ensemble spielen.

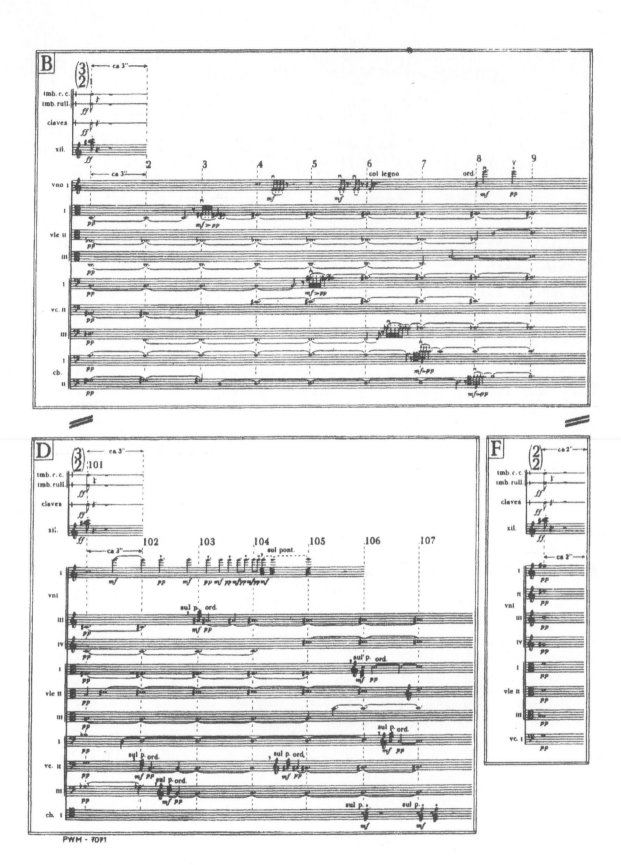

PWM - 7071

32. György Ligeti (1923-2006)
Ramifications, mm. 1-44 (1968-69)

*) The instruments in Group I sound a quarter-tone higher than written.
**) Double bass: it is written in the usual octave transposition, with exception of the natural harmonics, which are written as they sound ("SUONI REALI"). Concerning the artificial harmonics: their touch is written in the octave transposition, their resulting tone as it sounds.
*) Die Instrumente in Gruppe I klingen einen Viertelton höher als notiert.
**) Kontrabaß: in der üblichen Oktaventransposition notiert mit Ausnahme der natürlichen Flageoletts, die wie notiert klingen ("SUONI REALI"). Was die künstlichen Flageoletts betrifft, ist die Griffschrift in der Oktav-Transposition notiert, der sich aus ihr ergebende Ton so wie er klingt.

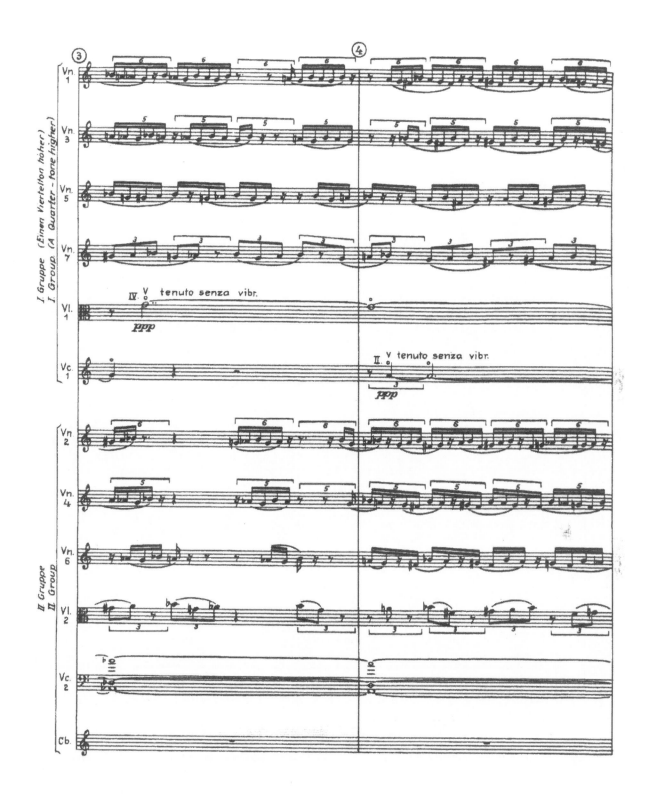

117

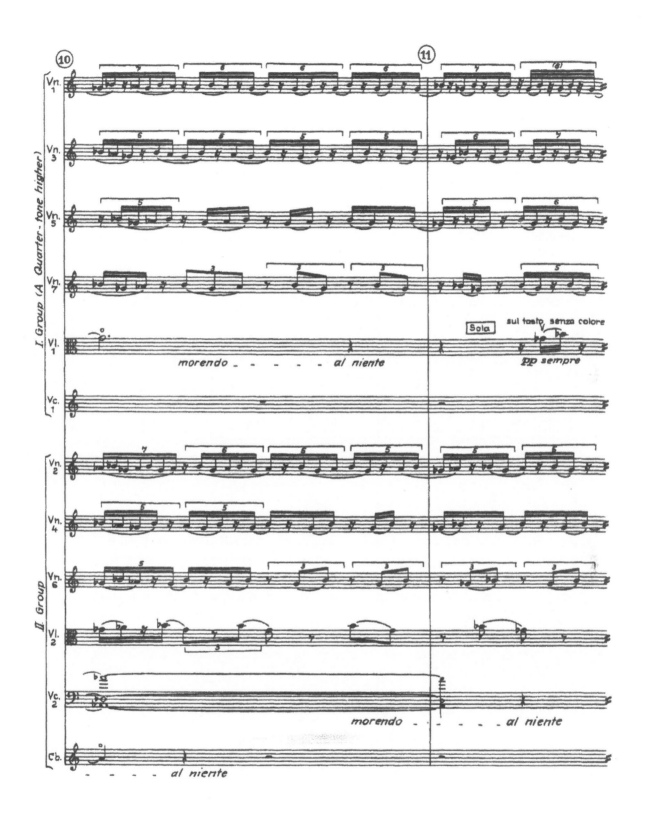

124

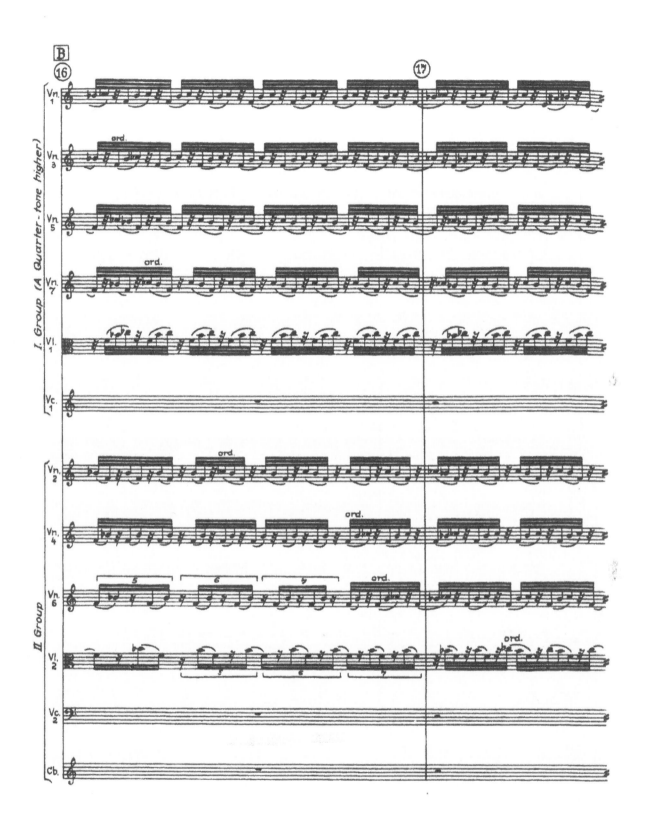

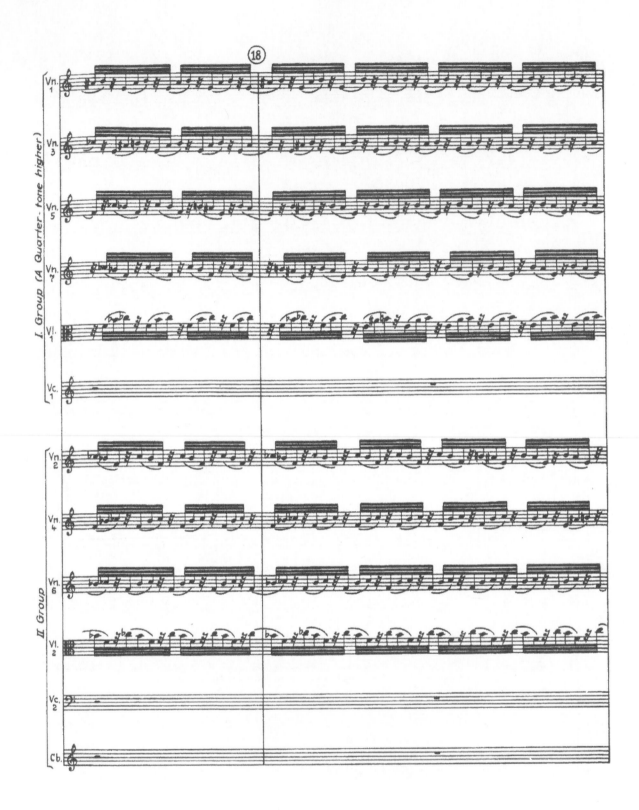

126

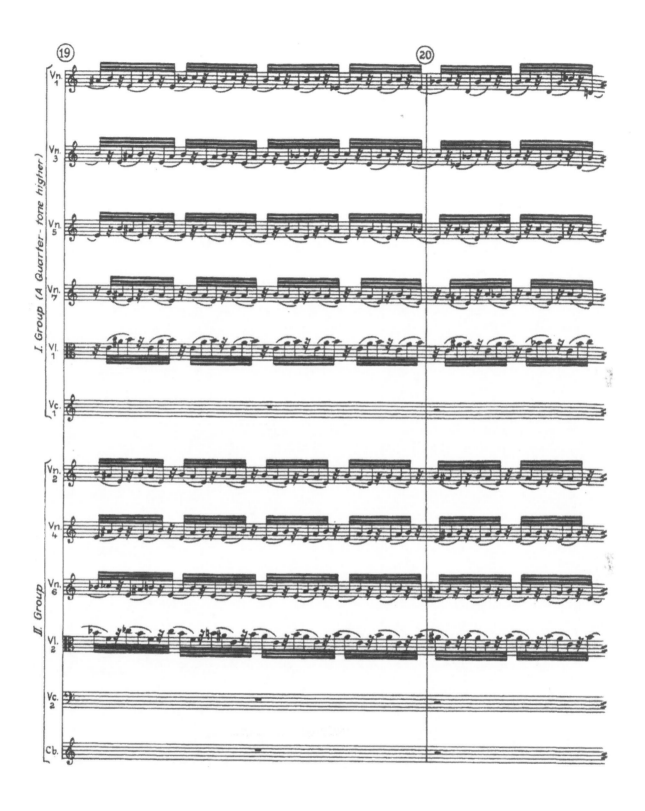

127

131

132

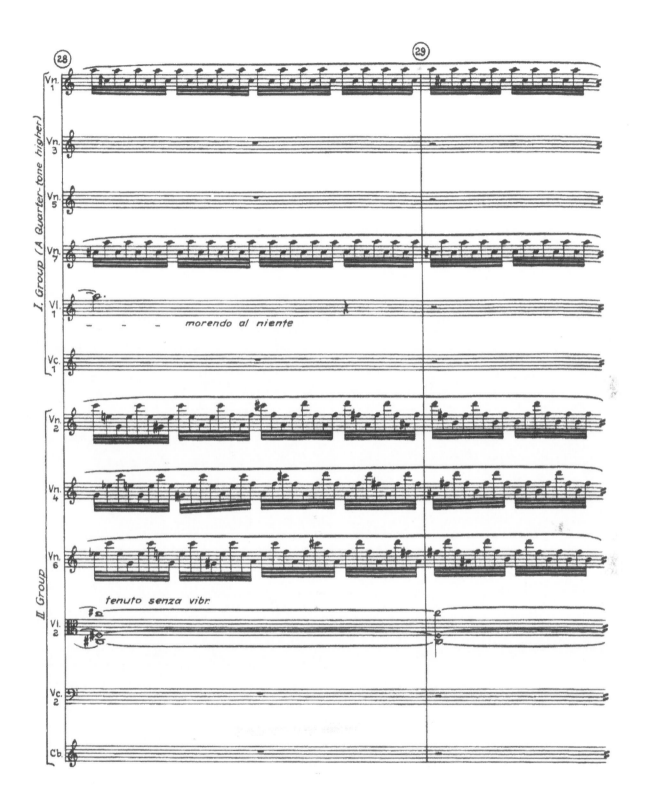

133

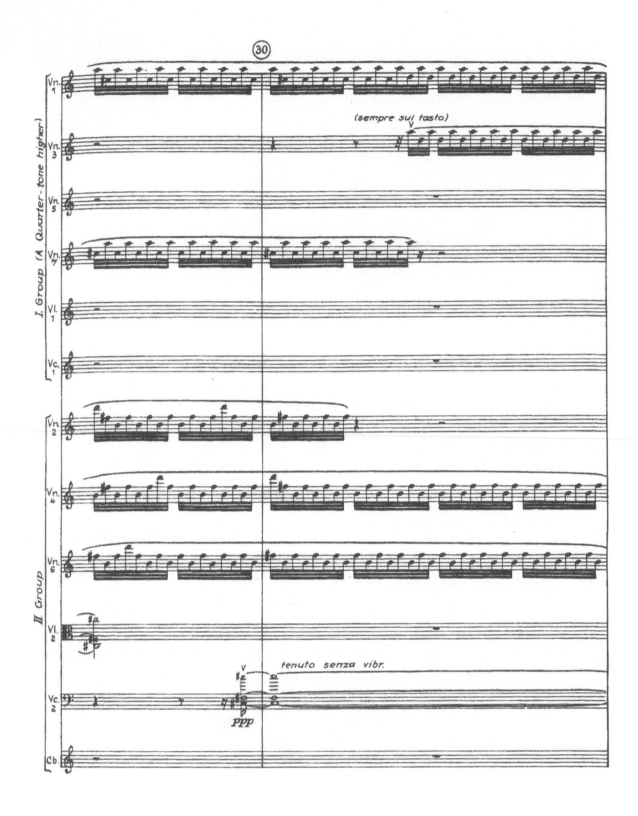

134

135

*) *All the tremoli in this piece: as thick as possible*
Alle Tremoli in diesem Stück: so dicht wie möglich

136

*) All the tremoli in this piece: as thick as possible.
* *) Double bass = touch: in the usual (transposed) notation; resulting tone: suono reale.
*) Alle Tremoli in diesem Stück: so dicht wie möglich.
* *) Kontrabaß: = Griff: in der üblichen (transponierten) Notierung; resultierender Ton: suono reale.

*) All the tremoli in this piece: as thick as possible.
  Alle Tremoli in diesem Stück: so dicht wie möglich.

33. George Rochberg (1918-2005)

Music for the Magic Theater, reh. 1-17 (1965)

N.B.: All instruments in this score are notated in C.

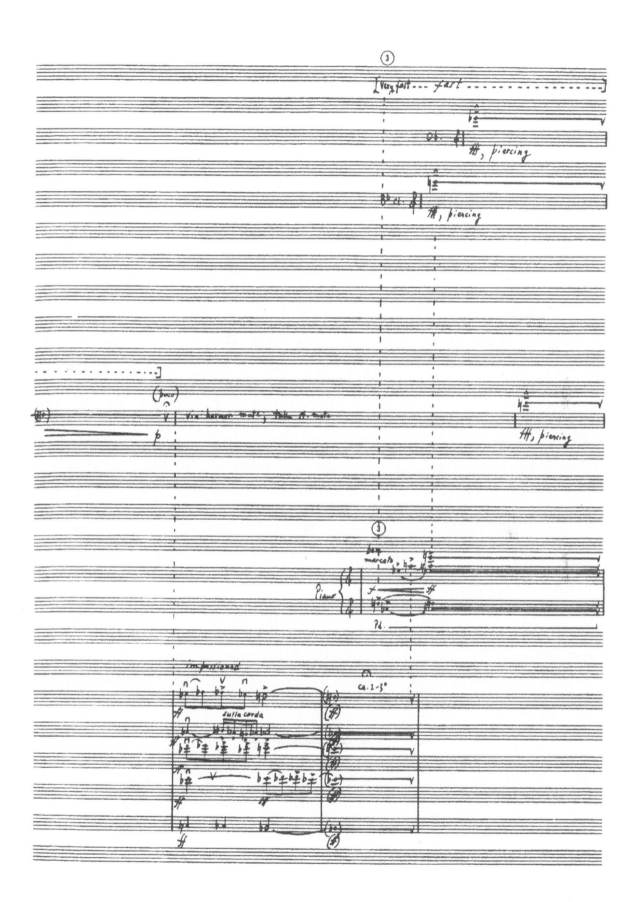

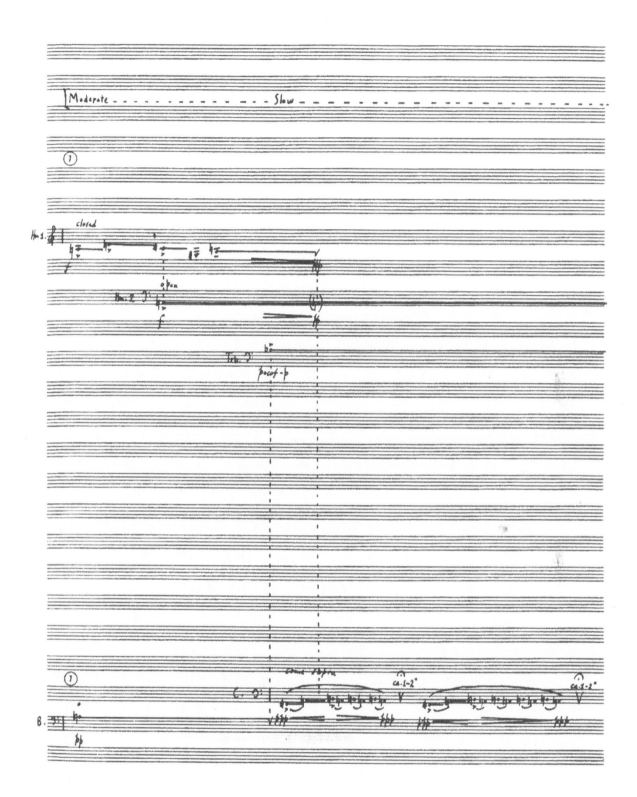

147

148

149

154

155

156

34. Luciano Berio (1925-2003)

Sinfonia, III ("In ruhig fliessender Bewegung"), mm. 1-120 (to reh. F) (1968)

N.B.: All instruments in this score are notated in C.

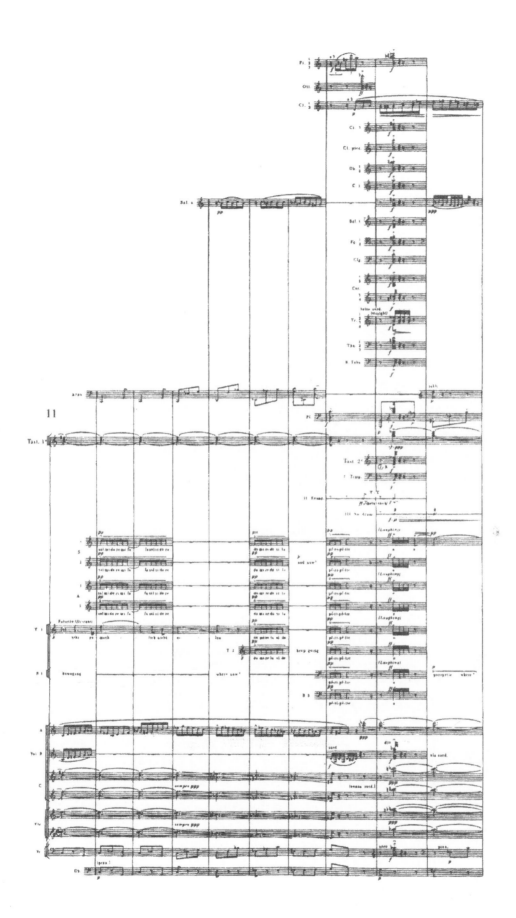

21

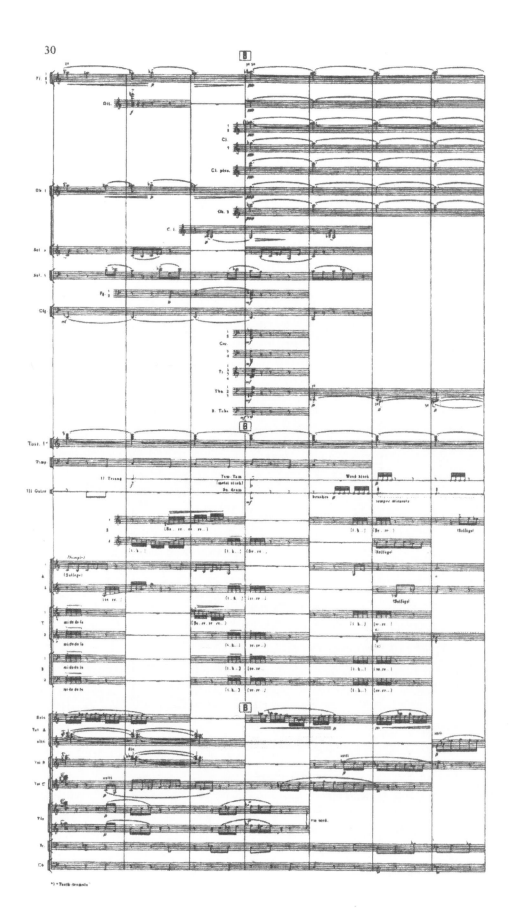

44

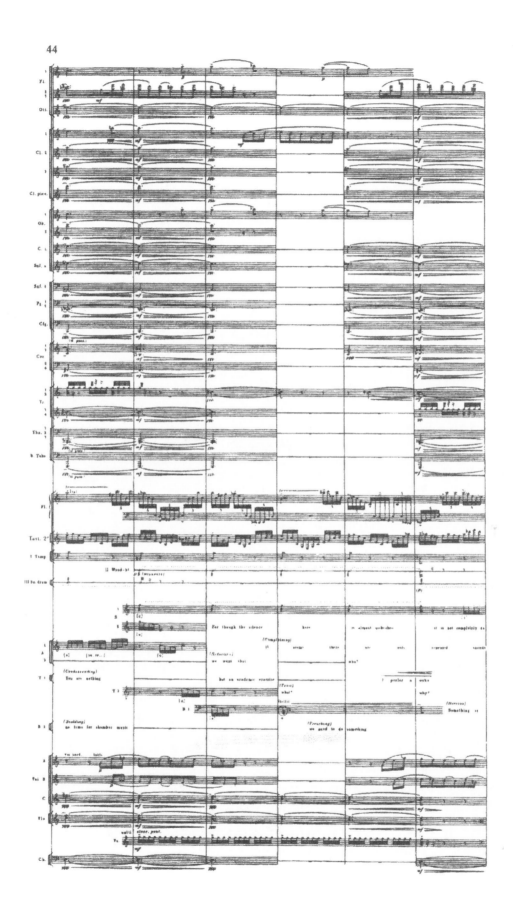

163

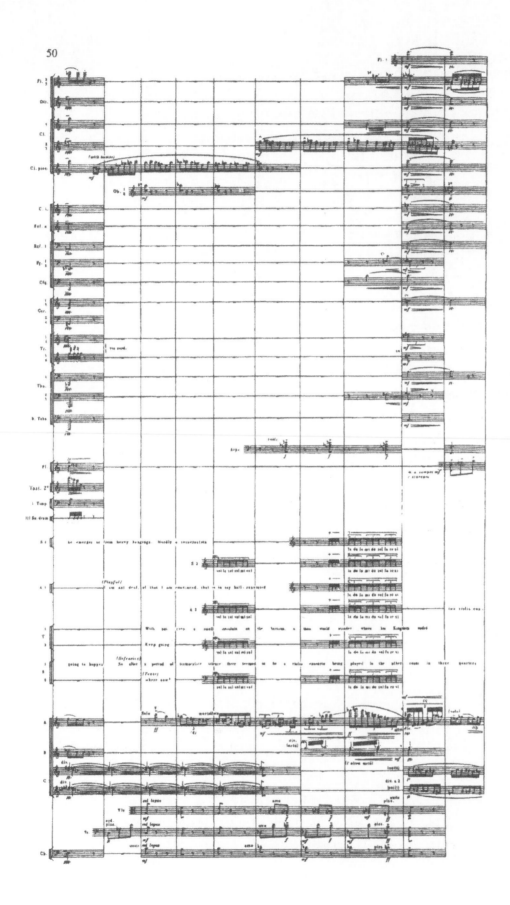

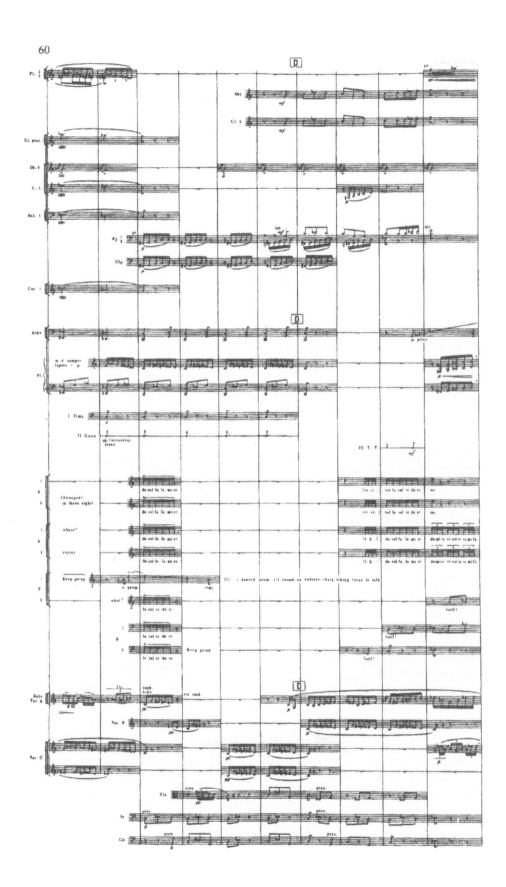

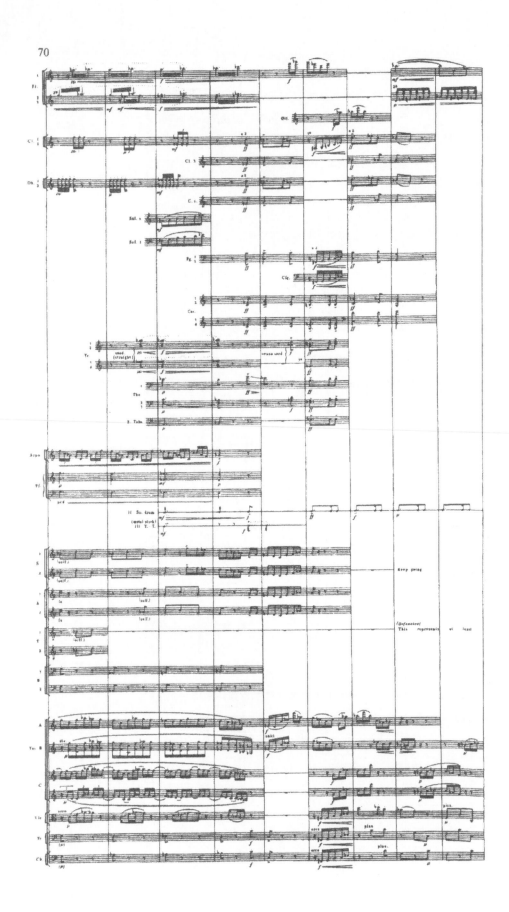

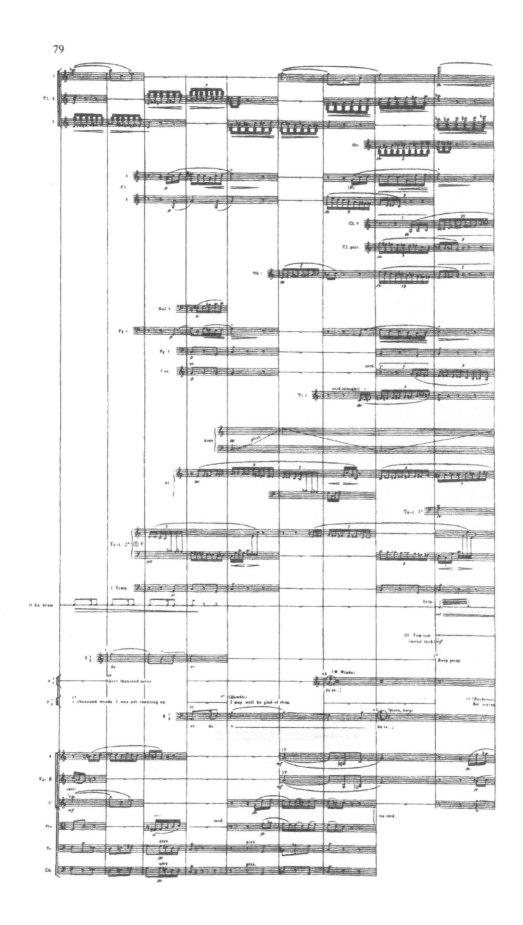

79

167

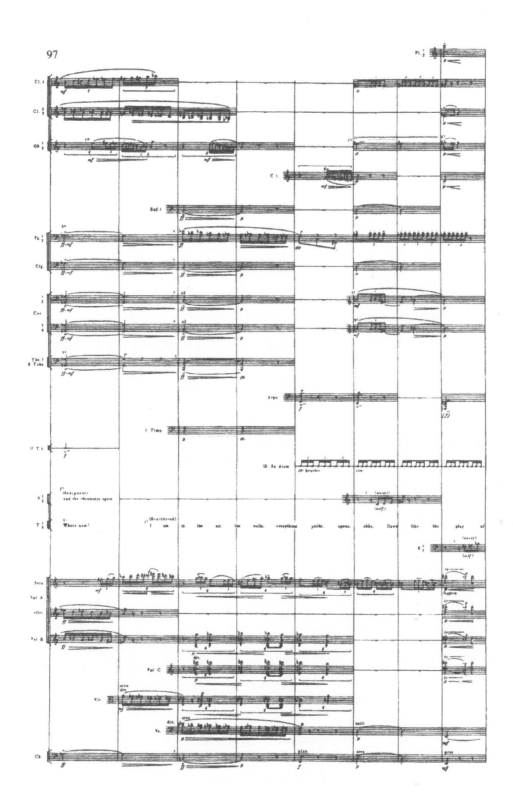

105

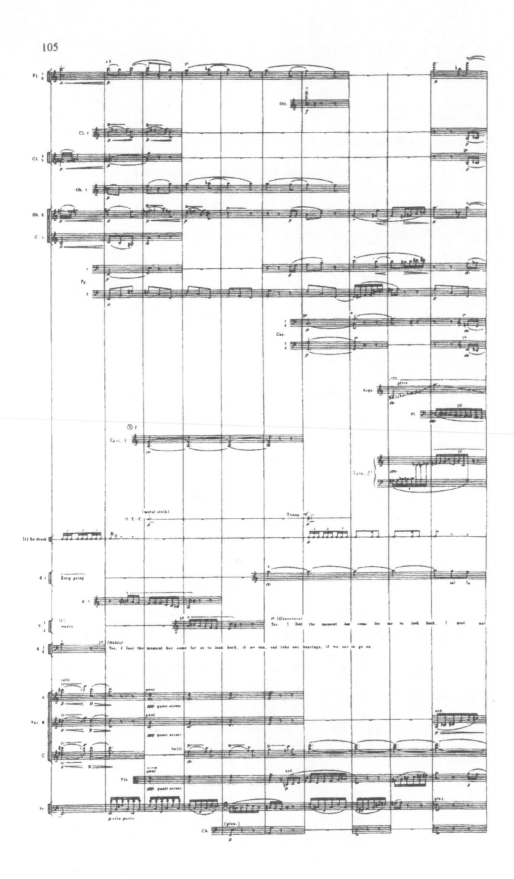

170

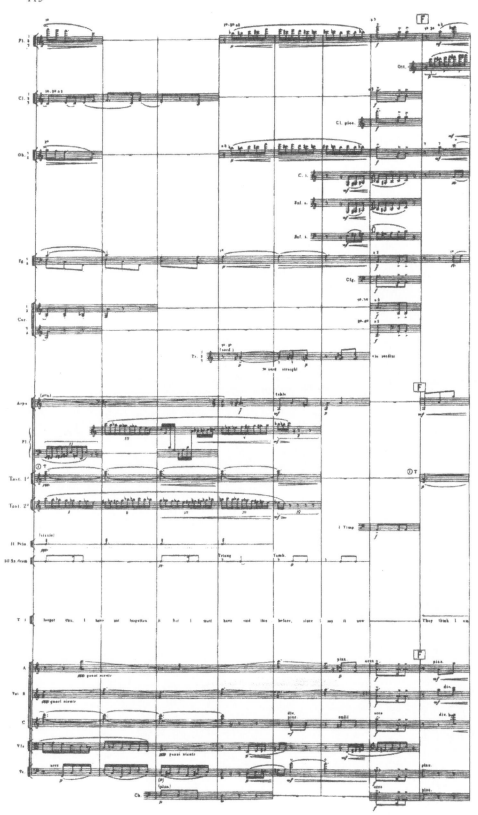

35. George Crumb (b. 1923)

"Dream Images (Love-Death Music)," no. 11 from *Makrokosmos*, vol. 1 (1972-73)

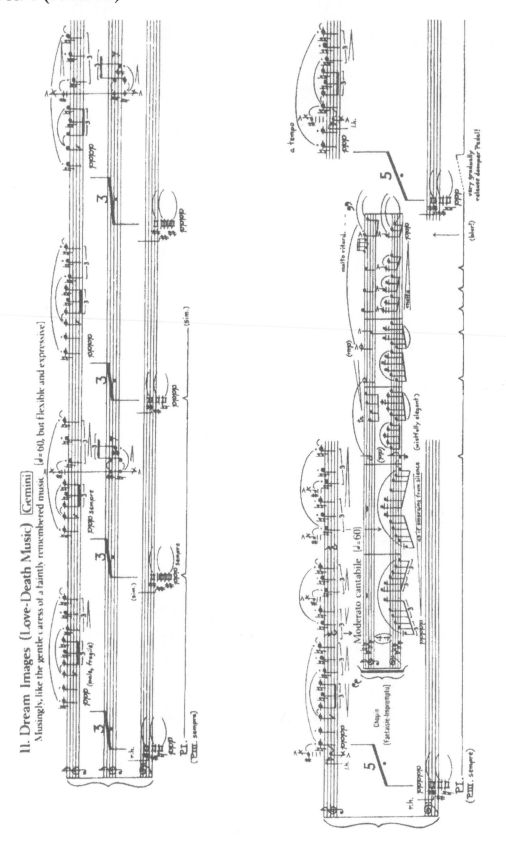

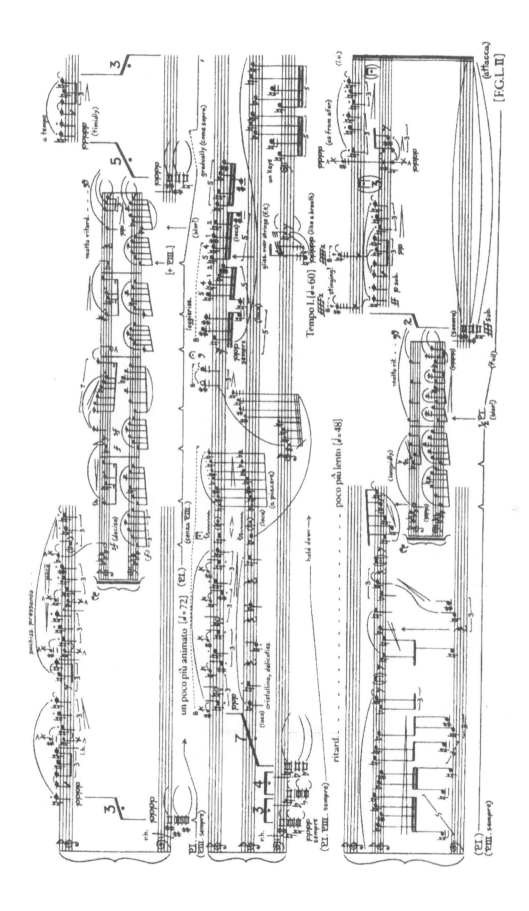

173

36. Steve Reich (b. 1936)
Violin Phase (1967)

176

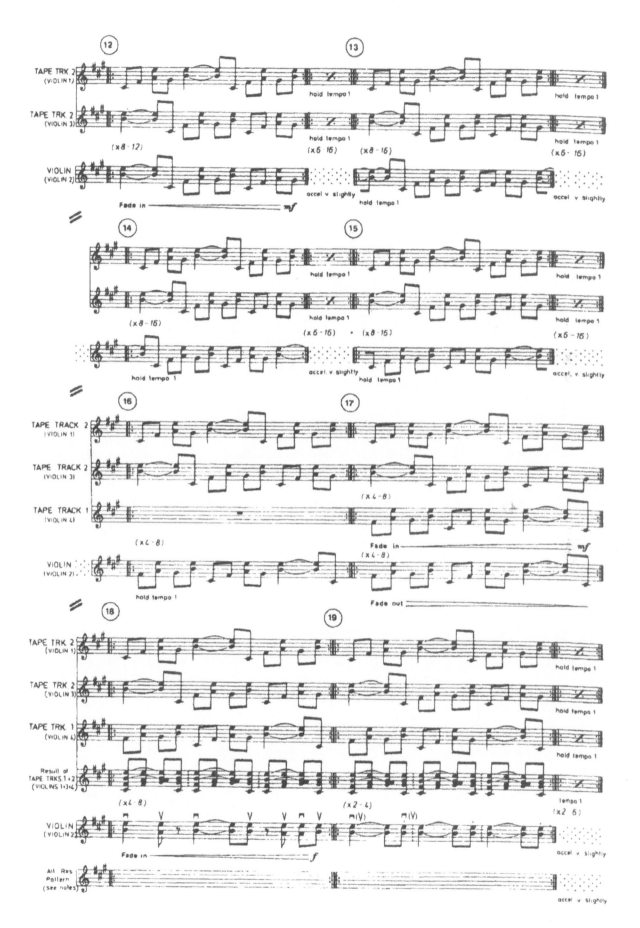

177

37. Louis Andriessen (b. 1939)
De Staat, mm. 1-161 (1972-76)

N.B.: All instruments in this score are notated in C.

183

185

ni - ān kai rhüth - mon tē lek - sei, o - li - gū pros tēn au-

191

*) no accent on low g

38. Arvo Pärt (b. 1935)
Cantus (1977)

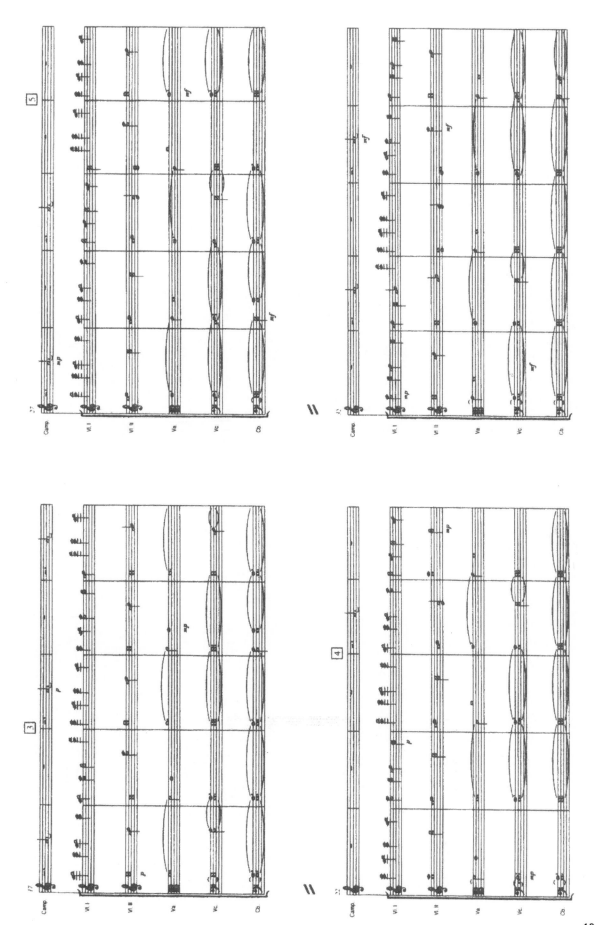

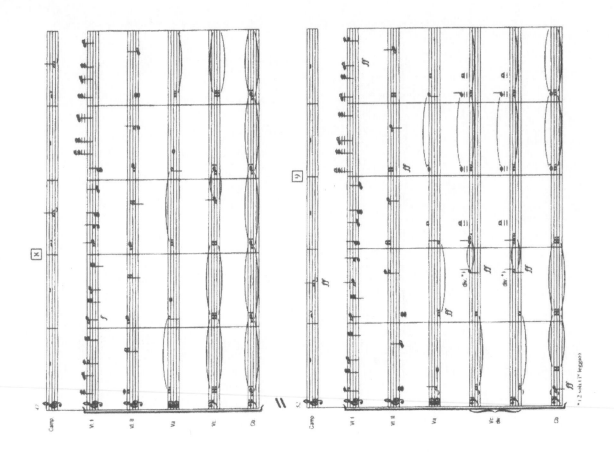

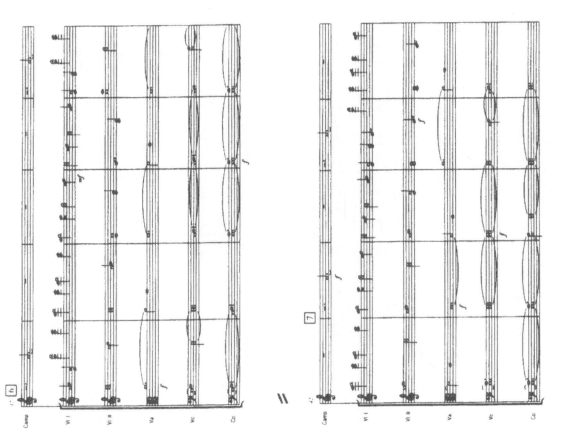

196

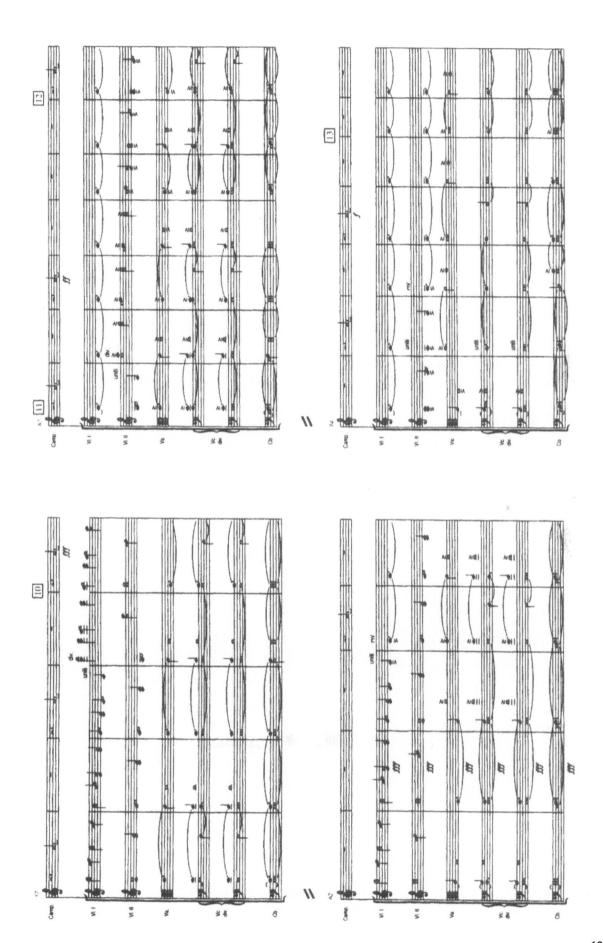

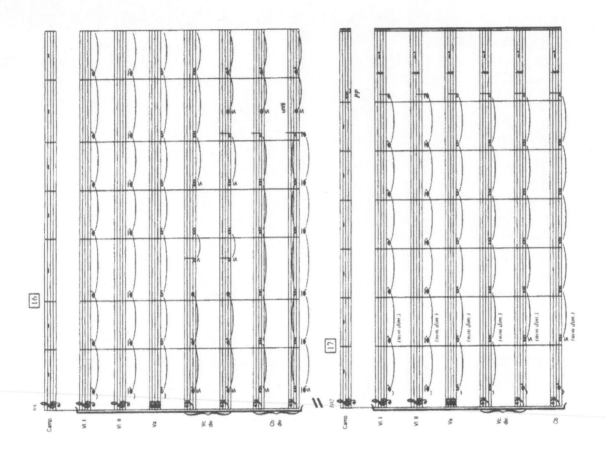

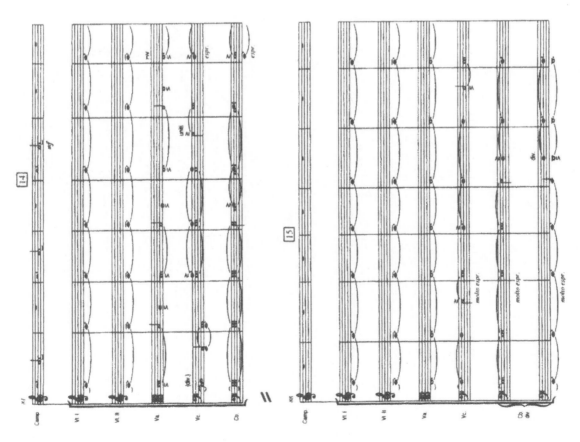

39. Augusta Read Thomas (b. 1964)
Spring Song, mm. 1-41 (1995)

*Play measures 16-33 as one long phrase, with subphrases of measures 16-24, 25-27, 28-30, 31, and 32.

40. Thomas Adès (b. 1971)
Asyla, II, mm. 1-43 (1997)

N.B.: All instruments in this score are notated in C.

205

41. Kaija Saariaho (b. 1952)
Ariel's Hail (2000)

Paris, 17 Sept. 2000

Acknowledgment of Sources